CU00659632

BEADING AND BONDING
IN
RIBBON EMBROIDERY

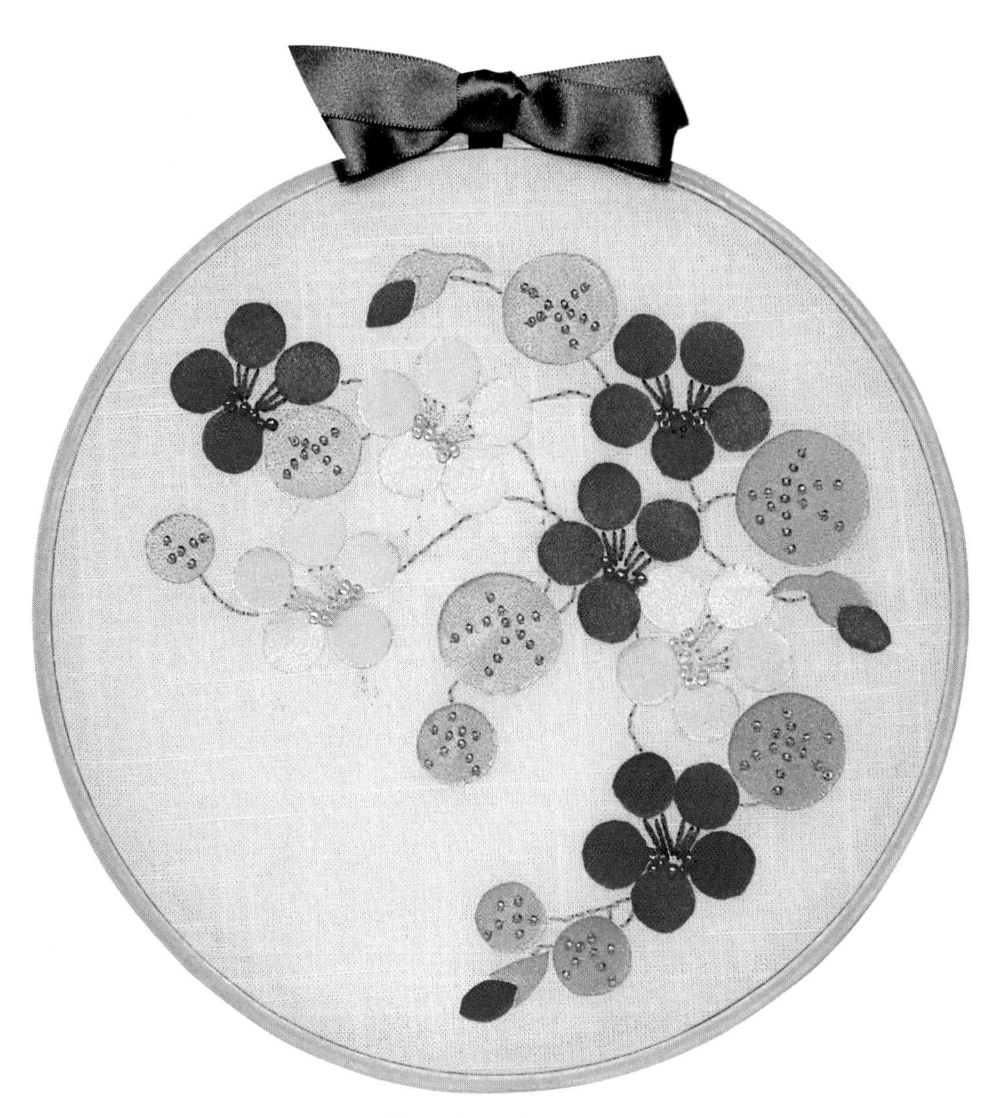

Nasturtiums (page 18)

BEADING AND BONDING IN RIBBON EMBROIDERY

Joyce Randall

Kangaroo Press

First published in 1993 by Kangaroo Press Pty Ltd
3 Whitehall Road Kenthurst NSW 2156
P.O. Box 6125 Dural Delivery Centre NSW 2158 Australia
Typeset by G.T. Setters Pty Limited
Printed in Hong Kong through Colorcraft Ltd

ISBN 0 86417 563 9

Contents

Waterlilies (page 42)

Introduction

This book contains original ideas and designs using beads, bonding, embroidery and painting on fabric. Through knowledge of one form of art or craft one discovers many things about others and is led to trying different mediums and techniques. A passion for colour can be kindled which is never extinguished.

Inspiration for this work came after a frenzy of ribbon embroidery. Beading, being back in vogue, was added. Fabric painting also seemed to combine well. Then bonding overcame certain difficulties posed by appliqué —and so it can go on.

Practical uses

The designs are shown in frames which keep the fabric taut for ease of sewing. Some are plastic frames and some are wooden embroidery hoops which can be used in the finished product with charming effects. The light coloured wood looks quite dainty finished with a ribbon bow to cover the screw, or can be covered by binding with ribbon.

In addition to framed pictures the designs can be used in many other ways:

Clothing—on pockets, collars, cuffs, belts, ties, gloves and hairbands, on yokes or necklines of blouses or dresses, on borders or to cover lengthened hems; on shawls, evening wear such as tops, boleros and waistcoats.

Accessories—evening bags, handbags, drawstring bags and soft scuffs.

Household linen—cushion covers, dressing table sets, table mats and runners, decorative corners and borders on curtains, bedspreads and tablecloths.

Decorative items—wall hangings and panels, bellpulls and box tops.

Be creative

If you feel beading is not appropriate on something you have in mind then substitute embroidery; perhaps use appliqué instead of bonding, bonding instead of painting or painting for bonding. Use different colours or materials and different shapes; enlarge or extend the designs to make wall hangings. Use part of a design only—maybe just a flower and leaf or a butterfly. Let your imagination lead you on.

There are twenty-two different designs and outlines for tracing in this book. I hope they will encourage ideas of your own which could be quite different from those illustrated.

Materials

Ways of approaching these designs and the materials needed are included in the instructions for each one. Fabrics used as bases are a firm cotton, fine linen, moiré and slub taffeta and crinkled polyester. Material for bonding is mainly satin ribbon.

Transferring designs

To transfer a traced design to the fabric, pin the design in place and slip a piece of graphite paper (obtainable at art shops), shiny side down, between design and fabric. Pin this in place also to prevent it rubbing on the fabric. Use a fine pointed biro to go over the design. This is best done on a hard surface. If you are using a frame, position the fabric in the frame first as it is difficult to get fabric in position after the tracing has been done, and smudging may occur. Find a smooth lid from a jar, or something similar, that can be placed underneath. Afterwards, if necessary, deepen outlines slightly with pencil, but don't make them too dark and obvious. White graphite paper is also available and can be used on coloured fabric.

Alternatively, trace the design onto paper, then pierce holes in the paper with a stiletto or fine sharp skewer at points such as petal tips and centres of the main flowers. Using a fade-out pen mark these points on the fabric through the holes. Use a white pencil on coloured fabrics. Embroider these design elements first, as penwork may fade in an hour or so. Do the same with the second most important flowers and so on.

Making up your own floral designs

If you want to make up your own floral design follow a similar procedure. Mark the positions of three main flowers, usually the largest, and complete these first, as often they take up more room than expected. Using the fade-out pen try marking in secondary flowers and when you are satisfied work these too. Do the same with leaves, and then mark in stems to make the design flow. To fill out the design, use French knots to represent tiny flowers. Remember that uneven numbers of flowers usually look better.

Bonding

To make many of the designs in this book you will need bonding paper (transfer fusing web), usually available from dress fabric or craft shops. The type used in these designs had web attached to one side of the paper only. Do not separate it. Glad Bake from the plastic wrap section of your supermarket is also necessary. Only the cut-out fabric shapes are bonded.

Protect your ironing board with a piece of Glad Bake.

Cut only enough transfer fusing web to hold the pieces to be bonded and place it paper side down and web side up on the Glad Bake.

Arrange the cut-out design pieces right side up and close together on top of the web.

Cover with a second piece of Glad Bake to prevent the iron sticking to web, and press well with a moderate heat.

Carefully peel paper off the back of the web, keeping everything flat. If the paper is allowed to twist you will end up with everything horribly stuck together. Tear off one piece at a time and trim with scissors.

Alternatively, a piece of material may be bonded to transfer fusing web and then shapes cut out. Peel paper from back of shapes afterwards.

Now place the background fabric on top of the Glad Bake on the ironing board, right side up, and put the design pieces in position, right side up.

Being careful not to move any of the pieces and spoil the design, lay Glad Bake on top and press well with iron.

Helpful hints

Fabric paint

Mix fabric paints with a little water and print paste reducer. They dry quickly like acrylics but will keep on a plate covered with plastic for two or three days. When using fabric paints for a background on fabric always cover an area larger than the frame it has to go into. Do not put the fabric in the frame before you paint it—remember it must be ironed to fix the paint. Do this with the fabric face down on brown paper.

Flat brushes ¼″ and ½″ wide are useful sizes for painting.

Lining

If you are using a thin fabric or a large frame, it is a good idea to line the fabric to keep it firm in the frame. A piece of white or matching lawn the same size can be used under silk or polyester. Flannelette is especially good in large wooden frames.

If the embroidery fabric is flimsy or likely to tear or shred it is essential to use a lining to facilitate drawing in to finish off the back. A lining may not be necessary if a frame is not to be part of the finished product, but may be used for such things as dress yokes, cuffs, belts and pockets. A coloured lining under a thin or transparent material can look pretty.

Tracing

When tracing a design onto your work trace inside the outlines of shapes which are to be covered by bonding or ribbon. This lessens the risk of lines showing.

Hoops

A wooden hoop is useful for working large pieces, as it can be moved around. It may not be suitable, however, if beading or bonding are being employed. The hoop cannot be moved around over beads and can sometimes disturb bonding.

Binding

When binding a frame with ribbon a small dab of craft glue will hold ribbon in place when starting and finishing.

Finishing

Do not glue felt to the back of a finished piece until you are satisfied that the work is padded sufficiently and has been drawn in and secured firmly.

Bonding

Use *only* Glad Bake paper over and under work when bonding with transfer fusing web. Glad Bake prevents the web sticking to iron or board. Most other papers will stick. Do practise with scraps first to become proficient.

Ribbon

Satin blanket ribbon binding can substitute for wide ribbon.

Washing

If fabric is washable use very gentle handwashing with no squeezing and iron face down on a soft towel. Use fabric painting or appliqué in preference to bonding on items that may need to be washed regularly.

Large pieces, like curtains, can be washed in the bath using a mild washing powder and warm water. *Do not rub.* Soak for a short time and then, holding by one end, gently pull from one end of the bath to the other, repeating several times. *Do not wring.* Rinse in cold water and hang in the shade while still dripping.

Ribbon embroidery

Silk ribbon

When working with silk ribbon, use lengths no longer than 22 cm, as the ribbon can fray at the edges before a longer length is used up. Pulling the ribbon through the material slowly helps prevent fraying. Keep ribbon flat.

Needles

- For use with small beads—quilting needles (No. 10).
- For embroidery cotton or silk—crewel needles.
- For ribbon embroidery—chenille needles—fine for silk ribbon, thicker for satin and wider nylon.

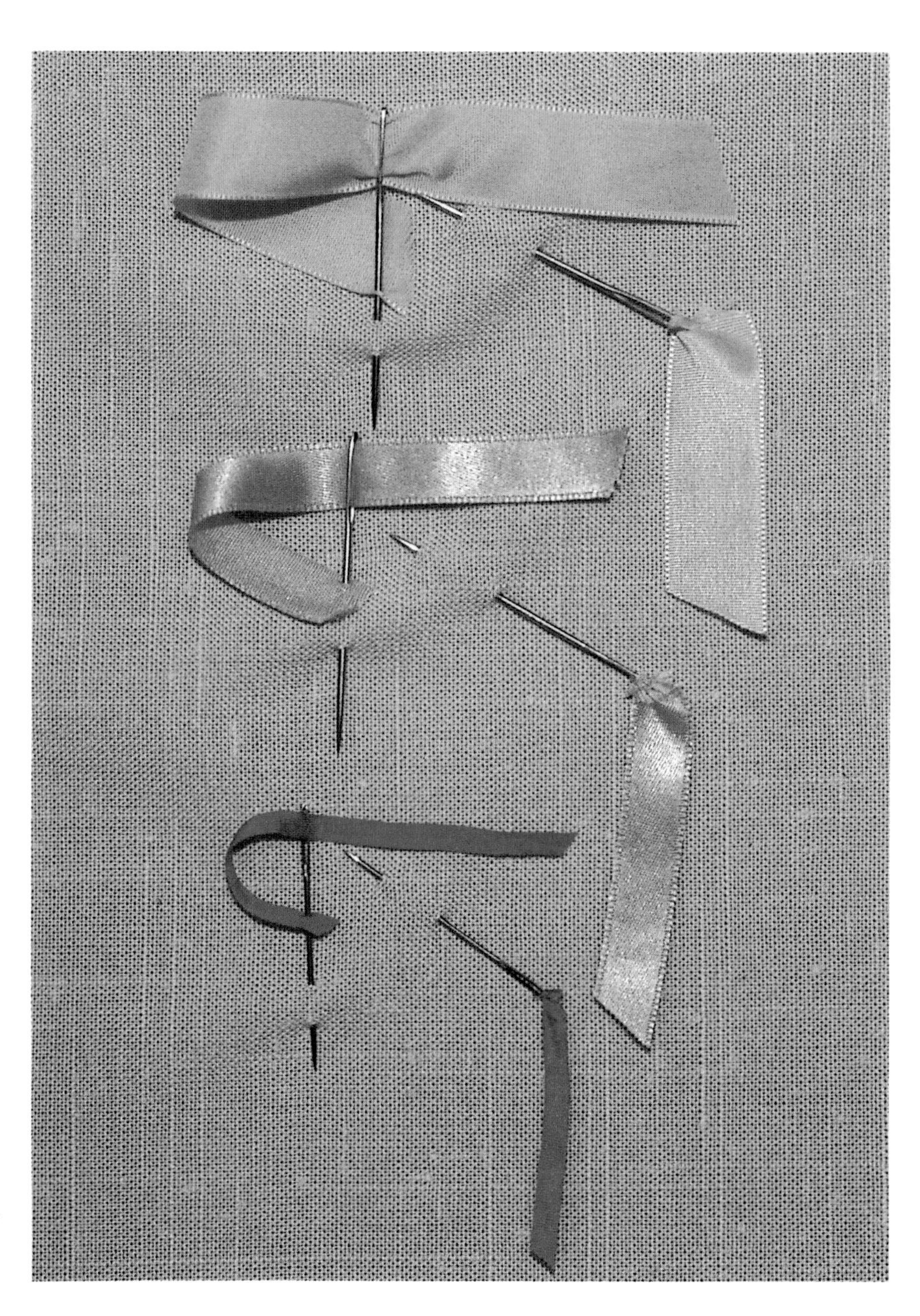

Threading the needle: the needles on the left show diagonally cut nylon taffeta, satin and silk ribbons with point threaded through needle and needle taken back through the ribbon near the tip; the needles on the right are ready for sewing

Threading the needle

Cut across the end of the ribbon diagonally before threading it. Push the pointed tip of the ribbon through the eye of the needle and pull about 2 cm through. Then push the point of the needle back through the ribbon, about 5 mm from the pointed tip. Pull the ribbon back through the needle so that not much more than the tip of the ribbon is left attached. This presents less bulk when pulling the ribbon through the material.

Thicker or wider ribbon

If you are using satin ribbon or wide nylon ribbon it is of great importance to lessen the obstruction caused when the ribbon reaches the hole in the fabric. To help overcome this push the point of the needle back through the ribbon 5 mm from the tip and close to the selvedge. The ribbon is stronger there. Pull the ribbon back through the needle and twist it backwards and forwards so that not much more than the tip of the ribbon is left attached. This presents less bulk when pulling the ribbon through the material.

Use a stiletto to gently enlarge the hole if necessary. I find pliers handy sometimes to pull the needle through but I use them only if I think the fabric can take it and when the bulk of the ribbon has been minimised as far as possible.

Starting off

When starting off leave 15 or 20 mm of ribbon at the back of the work. If fine silk or rayon ribbon is being used, the next stitch through to the back will often pierce the starting-off end and save finishing off. Do not do this with thicker ribbon as it does not pass through itself easily. Leave it hanging at the back to be sewn down later.

Finishing off

Take the ribbon through to the back and cut it about 1 cm from the work. You will probably have several cut-off pieces which will all need securing with needle and thread to stitches at the back of the embroidery. It is nearly impossible to keep the back of the work tidy.

Stitches

Much floral work can be accomplished using plain straight stitches and keeping the ribbon flat. Embroider most stems in stem stitch; back-stitch can be used for an attractive alternative. For a thicker stem these stitches can be 'whipped' by sewing a thread through each stitch afterwards. French knots are useful as small flowers to fill out a design. Fly stitch can also be used for this purpose and is good as a starting point when embroidering ribbon roses.

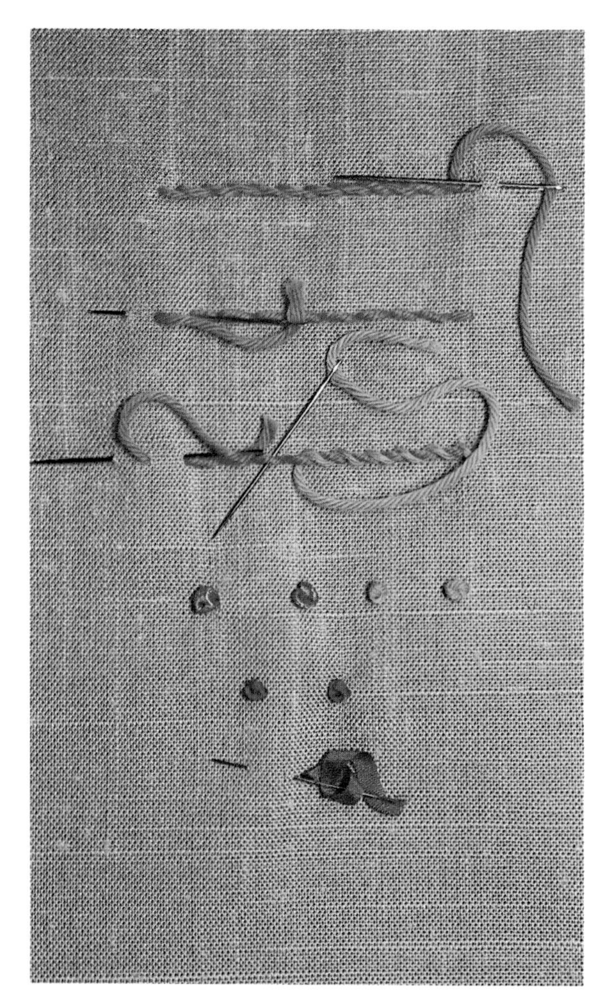

1. Stem stitch
2. Back stitch
3. Whipping
4,5. French knots
6. Making a French knot

1. Fly stitch—different ways
2. Making spokes of a wheel by starting with fly stitch
3. Bringing ribbon up next to centre and over and under spokes until spokes cannot be seen
4. Finished rose

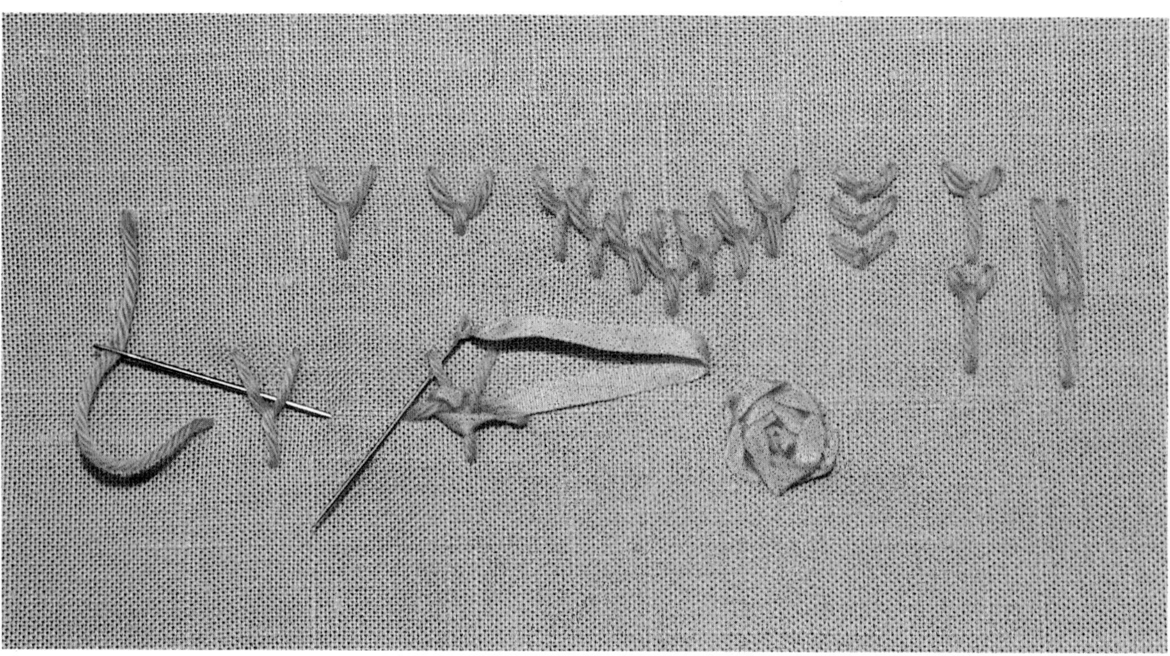

Folded roses

Folded roses can be used in designs for really pretty floral effect. A firm 7 mm satin ribbon is the best choice.

Take a length of ribbon and hold it vertically; about 14 cm up fold over horizontally to the right. Holding with the thumb, bring the short end up vertically, followed by the long end across to the left. Bring the short end down and the long end across to the right, and so on, until the short end is used up. Hold the end firmly with the thumb and first finger against the long piece of ribbon and let the folded part go. Still holding on, pull the long ribbon back carefully until the rose forms. Secure with a stitch down the middle and at the base. Trim ends and sew onto the design.

Steps in making a folded rose

Frames and hoops

The coloured plastic picture frames used in some of the illustrations here are wonderful for beginners and very easy to use. Each comes with an insert over which the fabric is placed. The insert slips into the frame, keeping the fabric taut while it is being embroidered. Each picture frame is its own embroidery hoop.

The wooden embroidery hoop, on the other hand, can be its own frame and looks quite dainty with a ribbon bow to cover the screw. Alternatively, the frame can be bound with ribbon for a very pretty effect as shown with some of the designs.

To do different parts of a very large embroidery the hoop may be moved around to different positions, but not if beads or bonding are being used.

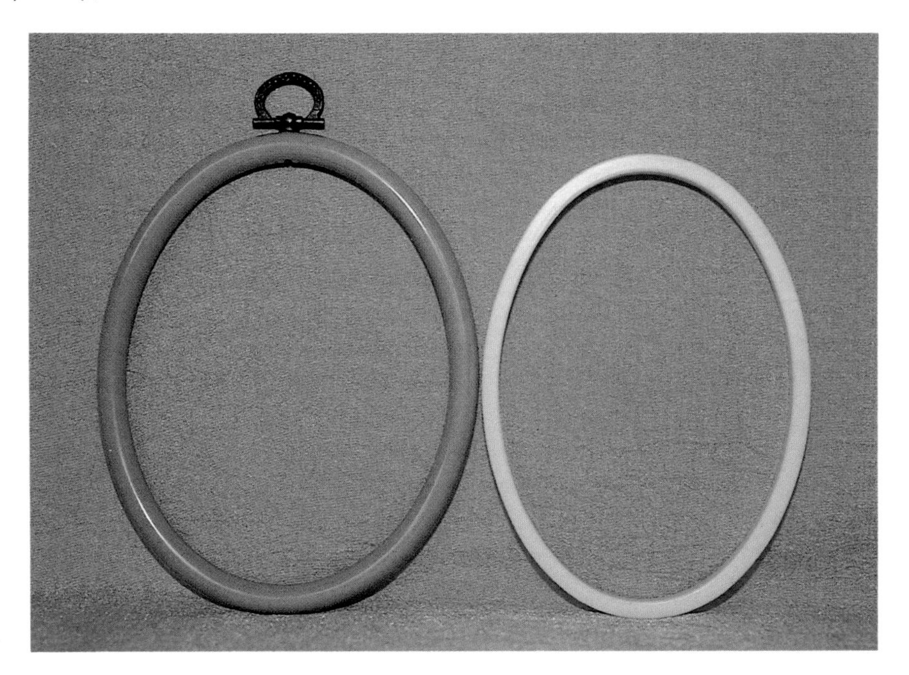

Plastic frame and insert

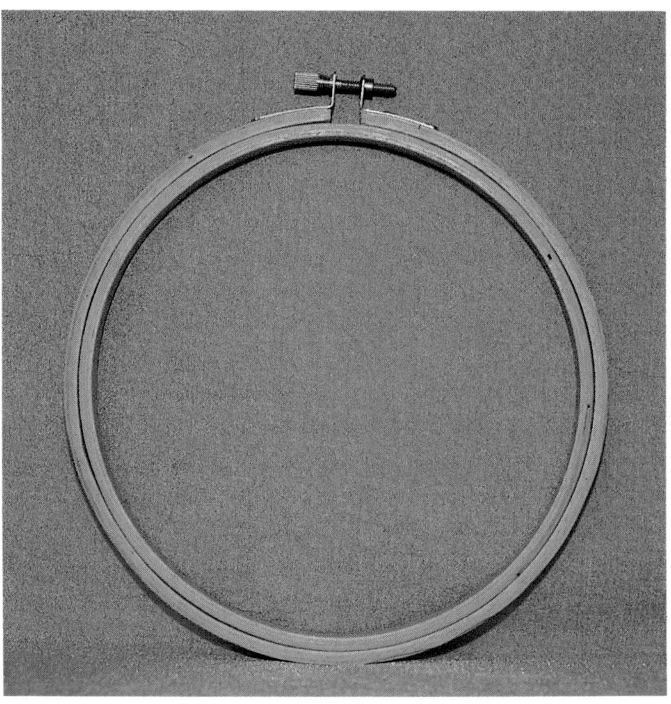

Wooden frame

Finishing off a framed embroidery

You will need:

A piece of strong cardboard cut to fit inside the frame insert
A piece of plastic foam the same size, about 8 mm thick
Cotton wool
Double thickness of white lawn or cotton fabric may be necessary, if white material is being used for the base of the design, to mask the colour of the plastic
A piece of felt to cover back

Turn the framed embroidery face down. Trim the fabric at the back leaving about 3 cm all the way around. Run a double thread of sewing cotton around the fabric, 1–1.5 cm from the raw edge, but do not finish off.

If cotton fabric is needed to mask plastic, cut it 5 mm larger than the inside measurement of the insert. Place the cotton fabric against the back of the embroidery. Over this put the plastic foam layer, then a layer of cotton wool, thicker in the centre, followed by the cardboard.

Hold the cardboard down while tightly drawing in the gathering thread around the raw edge of the embroidered fabric. Use two or three stitches to finish off the gathering thread. Thread the needle again with a double thread and zigzag across the back, working from side to side and end to end. Pull together as tightly as possible and finish off. Check that the cardboard is positioned level with the edge of the insert. It may be necessary to go around with another thread to tighten further.

Follow the same procedure for finishing the back of an embroidery in an embroidery hoop. If the frame is to be bound, loosen the screw at this stage and take out the embroidered centre. Bind the frame with 15 mm ribbon, starting at the screw and overlapping ribbon at each turn. Use a small dab of craft glue to hold in place. Return embroidery to frame and tighten screw well, using pliers if necessary.

To finish, cut a piece of felt the size of the frame, apply craft glue around the edge and stick to back of frame.

The surface of the picture can be protected with Scotchguard if you wish. Test on scraps of material first.

Lacing the back of the embroidery

THE DESIGNS

Nasturtiums

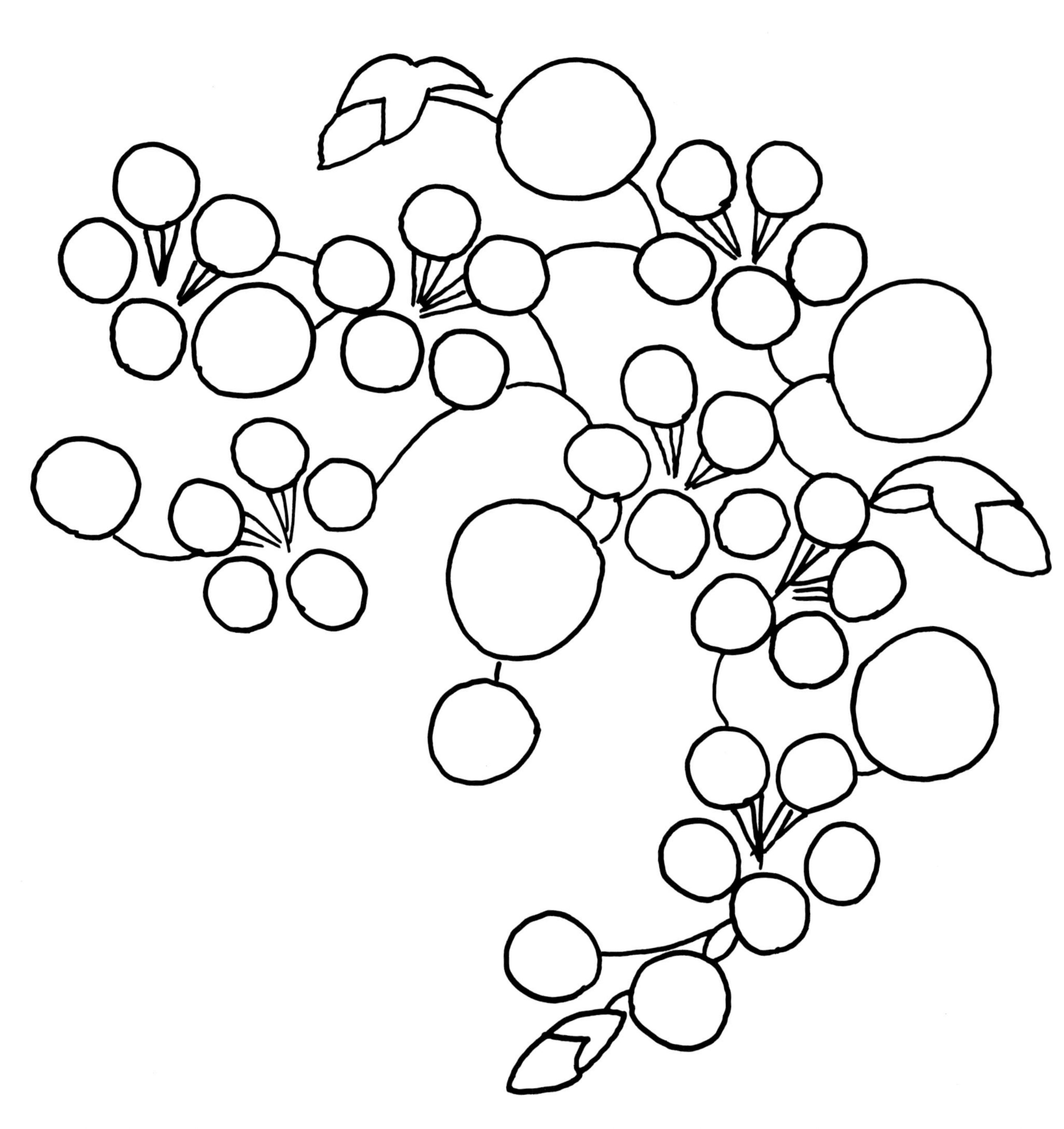

You will need:

21.5 cm wooden embroidery hoop
Cream linen cut 6 cm larger all round than frame
White lawn the same size for lining
17 mm satin ribbon in red and golden yellow
30 mm green satin ribbon
Red, green and yellow beads
17 mm satin ribbon in green for bow
Stranded cotton in matching colours

Lay linen and lawn together. Trace design and transfer to linen using graphite paper shiny side down and keeping inside the lines.

Mark circles on ribbon with white pencil, using coins, lids of small bottles or vials as guides—18 red in the same size, 15 yellow in the same size, and 9 green in different sizes. Mark 3 bud-shaped pieces in red.

Cut out all the circles and bud pieces and place right side up and close together on transfer fusing

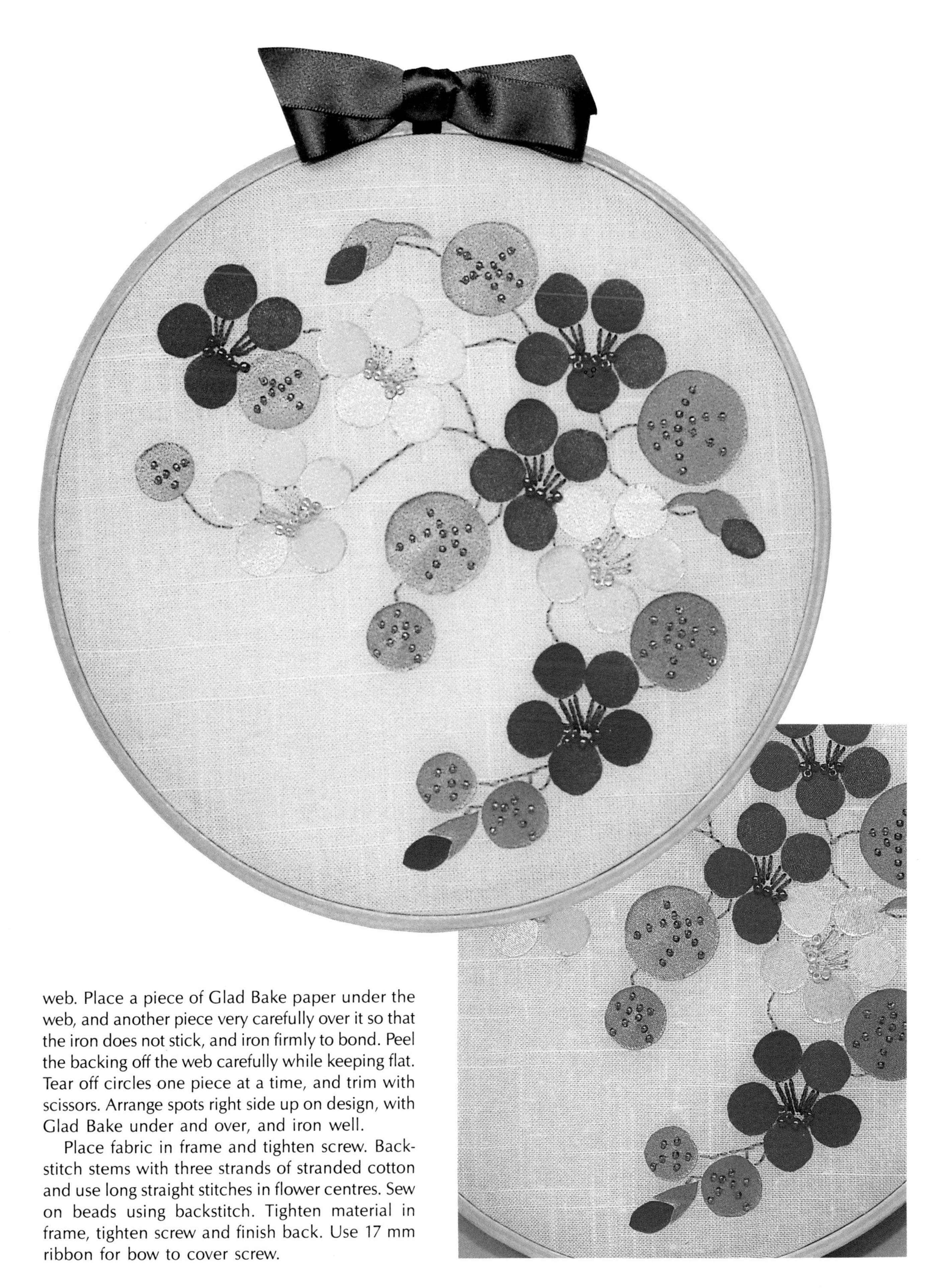

web. Place a piece of Glad Bake paper under the web, and another piece very carefully over it so that the iron does not stick, and iron firmly to bond. Peel the backing off the web carefully while keeping flat. Tear off circles one piece at a time, and trim with scissors. Arrange spots right side up on design, with Glad Bake under and over, and iron well.

Place fabric in frame and tighten screw. Backstitch stems with three strands of stranded cotton and use long straight stitches in flower centres. Sew on beads using backstitch. Tighten material in frame, tighten screw and finish back. Use 17 mm ribbon for bow to cover screw.

Butterflies

You will need:

21.5 cm wooden embroidery hoop
Pale blue crinkle polyester cut 6 cm larger than hoop all round
Lawn fabric the same size
Fine nylon net (optional) same size
Piece of blue satin blanket binding or very wide blue ribbon
Small piece of silver lamé
Lilac, light and dark blue and clear iridescent beads
3 metres dark blue 23 mm ribbon for binding frame and for bow

Trace design and pin in place on blue polyester. Slip graphite paper shiny side down in between. Trace butterflies only onto surface, keeping inside their outlines so that the graphite marks will not show later. Avoid pressing hard on paper with hands to keep work clean.

Trace and cut out butterfly shapes from blue satin and small body shapes from silver lamé. (If this is too difficult body shapes could be filled in with clear beads.)

Place all these pieces right side up and close together on transfer fusing web. Place Glad Bake under and very carefully over the fusing web so that

the iron will not stick, and iron firmly to bond. Peel the backing off the web carefully while keeping flat. Pull off one piece of fabric at a time and trim with scissors.

Arrange pieces right side up on design, with Glad Bake under and over, and iron well. Place silver bodies in place and iron on as well.

Lay the blue polyester and lawn together. If nylon net is being used place it over work and put the layers of fabric into position in frame. Pin tracing paper in position again (without graphite paper) and tack through it along feelers and joining lines. Tear paper away and the work is ready for beading. Use backstitch for beads on butterflies. With silver thread, backstitch next to the lines of tacking, attaching beads at intervals.

Remove tacking, tighten material in frame, tighten screw and finish work on back but do not glue on felt. Remove from frame for binding. Return to frame, tighten screw, glue on felt and tie bow to cover screw.

Raggedy roses

You will need:

21.5 cm wooden embroidery hoop
Pink crinkle polyester cut 5 cm larger all round than hoop
White lawn the same size for lining
About 10 cm each of dark red, pink, and grey-and-white striped crinkled polyester
Scraps of black material (moiré taffeta used here)
Black, pink and red beads

Cut three 8 cm circles of pale pink and striped fabric, and 4 circles of red. Turn edge of each circle over 0.5 cm and use a small running stitch to run a thread around each circle, but do not finish off. Draw thread in until there is another 0.5 cm turned under all round, and iron to flatten edge a little. Do this with each one.

Take about five long stitches on the wrong side of each circle (as shown in the small diagram), and draw in loosely to give the appearance of a flower.

Place one red circle in the centre of work and fix in place with two or three stitches near centre.

Note It is not really necessary or recommended that the design be traced, even though the outline is included. Tracing lines could be visible under flower edges where they kick up.

Arrange the other circles to overlap each other all around the central circle, and stitch in place. If necessary tiny stitches can be used to hold down some edges.

Cut out black leaf shapes and place right side up and close together on a piece of transfer fusing web with Glad Bake paper underneath and on top to prevent sticking. Iron well and then peel paper off back carefully, keeping work flat. Tear off leaves one at a time and trim with scissors. Tuck leaves around flowers as shown and with a piece of Glad Bake under the work and a small piece over the leaf, bond with the iron one at a time.

Lay the polyester and lawn together and put the work in the frame. Sew coloured beads in flower centres and black ones around leaves. Tighten work in frame and tighten screw. Finish off back and cover screw with bow.

Cinerarias

You will need:

21.5 cm wooden embroidery hoop
Fawn linen cut 6 cm larger than hoop all round
White lawn the same size for lining
3 mm satin ribbon in dark red, two pinks, blue, purple and green
6 mm green satin ribbon
20 mm green satin ribbon
16 mm ribbon for bow

Trace design, pin to fabric, slip graphite paper shiny side down in between and trace on, being careful not to press down and smudge graphite. Petals may be marked lightly with a single line. Place linen and lawn together and put into frame.

With 3 mm ribbon and straight stitches sew flower petals. Use French knots in centres.

Join pieces of wide green ribbon together with

tiny stitches to make centre veins of leaves and buttonhole onto design. Use narrow green ribbon for stems, leaving about 4 cm hanging down, and sew down with tiny stitches 2 or 3 cm apart. Small leaves are made with 6 mm ribbon. For the thin stems use 6 strands of stranded cotton and long stitches.

Tighten material in frame, gather, pad and secure back. Remove from frame, tuck ribbon ends in and return. Tighten screw, glue on felt and cover screw with ribbon bow.

Hydrangeas

You will need:

18.5 cm wooden embroidery hoop
Grey cotton fabric cut into circle 5 cm larger all round than frame
Fabric paint
3 mm silk ribbon in two pinks and two blues
Blue, pink and green beads
16 mm ribbon for bow

Trace design and transfer to fabric using graphite paper shiny side down. Mix suitable shades of pink, blue and green in fabric paint and apply to design with a flat ½″ brush. Allow to dry and iron face down on brown paper to fix colour.

Put fabric into frame. Sew flowers at random on patches of colour, using straight stitches left a little

loose. Put one matching bead in centre of each flower and outline each patch of colour with suitable coloured beads. Outline leaves and stems as shown.

Tighten fabric in frame, tighten screw and finish back. Tie ribbon bow to cover screw.

Bougainvillea collage

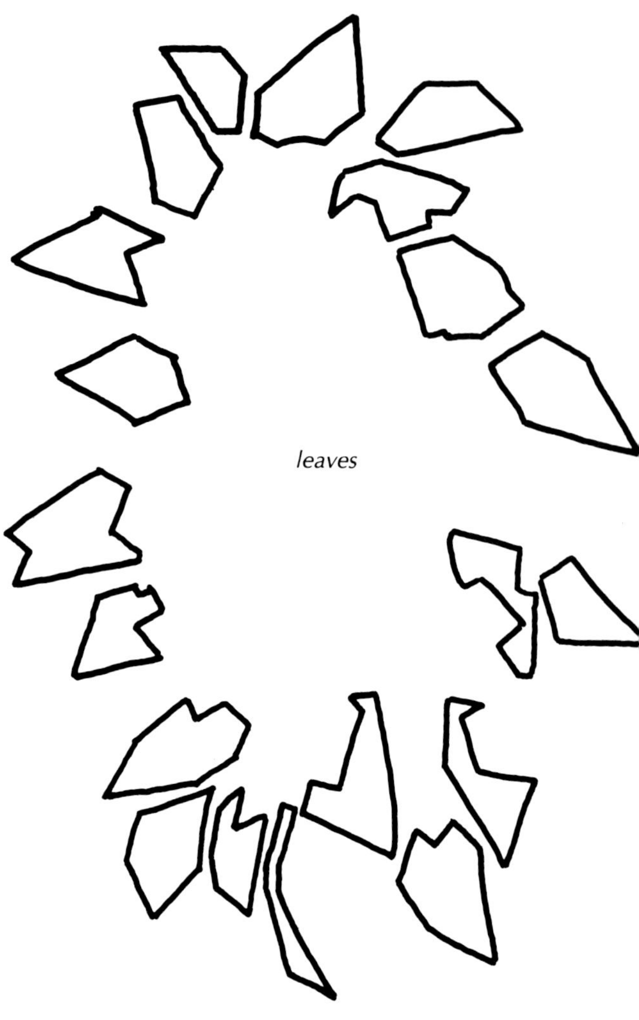

You will need:

Plastic frame 19.5 × 14 cm
Cream linen cut 3.5 cm larger all round than frame
White lawn fabric cut same size as linen
16 mm satin ribbon in three shades of green
25 mm satin ribbon in pink and cerise
Yellow beads

Pin traced design to linen and slip graphite paper shiny side down in between. To keep clean avoid pressing hard on paper with hands. Trace inside the lines.

Cut out leaf shapes from tracing paper, place them on ribbon, trace around with white pencil. Cut out inside white lines. Place ribbon leaf pieces right side up on transfer fusing web with Glad Bake paper underneath and on top to prevent sticking. Iron well and then carefully peel paper off back while keeping flat. Tear off one piece at a time and trim around with scissors. Place in leaf positions (as

shown in line drawings) on design. With Glad Bake in position as before iron to bond. Next cut out flower shapes, treating them the same way as leaves, and bond to design. Lay the lawn under the linen, put the work into the frame and sew the beads in place.

This is a little like a jigsaw puzzle and takes time and patience, but once the pieces are bonded in position and the beads sewn on the work is finished. Tighten material in frame and finish back.

Alternatively, do not trace design on to material but bond leaf and flower pieces in place to suit yourself, overlapping and using extra pieces if necessary.

Wildflowers

You will need:

16.5 cm wooden embroidery hoop
Fine linen fabric cut 5 cm larger all round than hoop
Fabric paint
3 mm satin ribbon in pink, white and three greens
6 mm satin ribbon in pink, pale yellow, golden yellow, dark red, mauve and violet
7 mm nylon ribbon in light blue and dark blue
16 mm green satin ribbon for bow

Mix small quantities of fabric paint to match the colours you have selected for the wildflowers. Paint linen with small patches of colour to correspond with the colours of the flowers. Use green paint in between where necessary. Allow to dry and then iron face down on brown paper to fix colour.

Put fabric into frame. All flowers are sewn using straight stitches and French knots where shown. Fit extra white clematis into any spaces between flowers. Do stems with backstitch and place leaves wherever there is room. Tighten fabric in frame, tighten screw and finish back. Tie on green ribbon bow to cover screw.

Black-eyed Susan

You will need:

11.5 × 15.5 cm plastic frame
Fine fawn coloured linen cut 4 cm larger all round than frame
White lawn the same size for lining
6 mm satin ribbon in pink

Place linen and lawn together and put into frame. Trace design onto tissue paper and transfer to linen using graphite paper shiny side down.

Flowers are made with straight stitches as shown. Use two or three stitches in black stranded cotton for centres. Backstitch stems and make small leaves with three strands of dark olive green stranded cotton. Tighten material in frame and finish back.

Hibbertia

You will need:

11.5 × 15.5 cm plastic frame
Grey cotton material cut 4 cm larger all round than frame
Fabric paints
Olive-green and orange embroidery cotton
10 mm satin ribbon in golden yellow

Using fabric paints mix yellow, green, grey and fawn and paint fabric. Dry well and iron the back over brown paper to fix colour. Put into frame, and apply traced design using graphite paper shiny side down.

Sew flowers with straight stitches, leaving the stitches very loose. Fix in place with tiny stitches if necessary. For centres make two or three French knots in orange embroidery cotton and do stems and leaves in olive colour. Tighten material in frame and finish back.

Fringed lilies

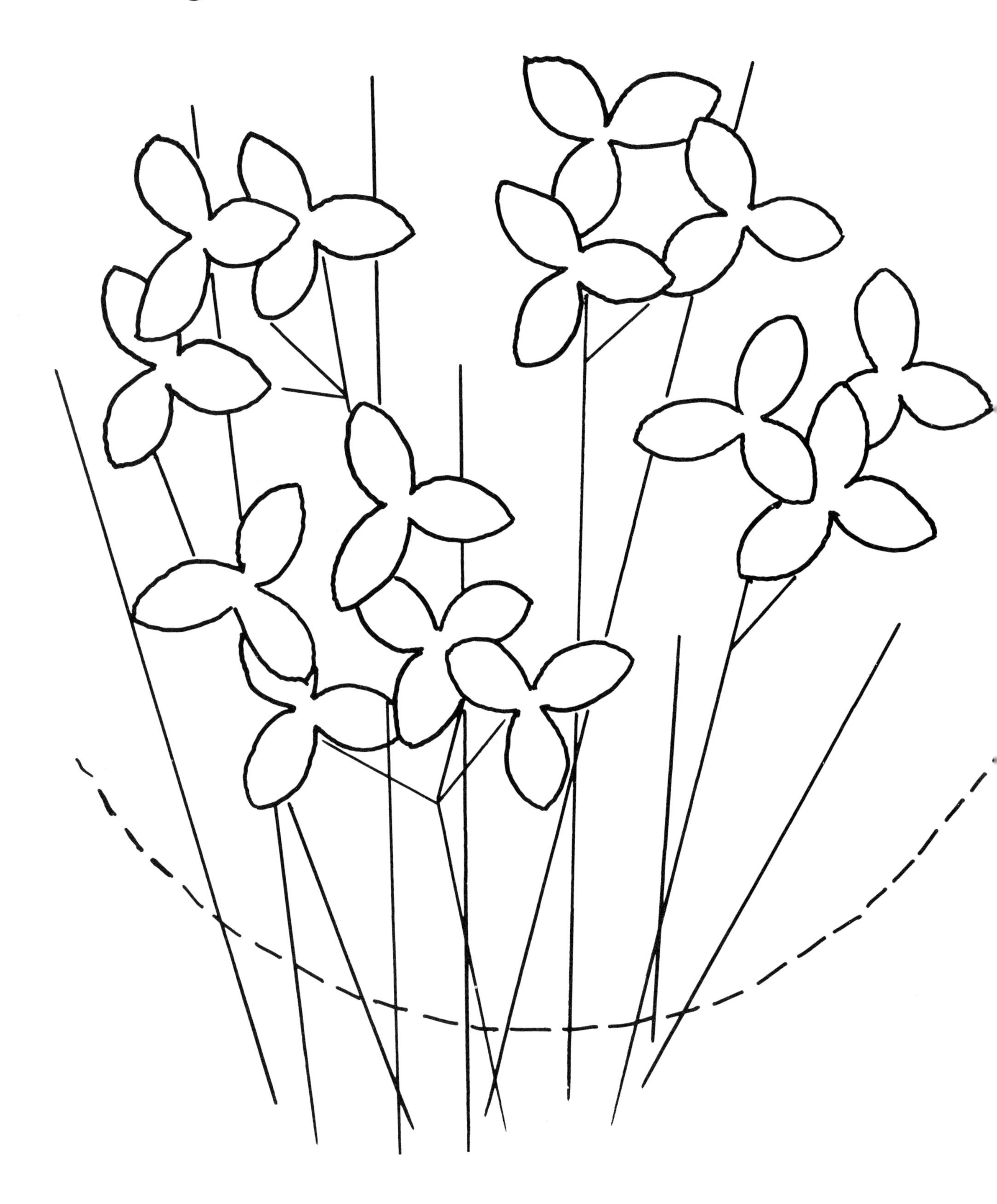

You will need:

21.5 cm wooden embroidery hoop
Cream fine linen cut 5 cm larger all round than frame
White lawn the same size for lining
Mauve satin blanket binding
3 mm satin ribbon in green and mauve
15 mm green velvet ribbon

Place linen and lawn together and put in frame. Apply traced design lightly using graphite paper shiny side down and keeping inside the lines. Cut 14 flower shapes from the mauve satin blanket binding, pin in place and satin stitch a little unevenly around edges. Sew three straight stitches in mauve ribbon to each flower. Work two French knots in each centre using green embroidery silk. Sew on beads. Use green ribbon for stems, allowing an extra 3 cm at bottom. Catch stems at intervals with tiny stitches and leave ends hanging loose.

Take work out of frame and bind frame with green velvet ribbon. Put frame back on, keeping stem ends tucked in. Pull linen tight, tighten screw and gather and secure back. Glue on felt. Use velvet ribbon bow to cover screw.

Constellation

You will need:

19.5 × 14 cm plastic frame
Black moiré taffeta cut 3.5 cm larger than frame all round
Lawn fabric cut same size
22 mm satin ribbon (very short lengths) in white and gold
Gold beads
Iridescent clear beads
Tiny pearl beads

Mark circles on 22 mm ribbon using coins, lids of small bottles or vials—one white and three gold. Cut out the circles inside the pencil lines and place right side up on a small piece of transfer fusing web with a piece of Glad Bake paper under and over, and iron well. Peel the backing off the web and tear off one circle at a time. Trim with scissors. Arrange spots right side up on the taffeta and with Glad Bake under the work and over pieces, iron to bond.

Lay taffeta over the lawn fabric and place work in frame. Backstitch 3 or 4 gold beads to centre of white spot and surround closely with a circle of pearl beads. With 2 strands of white stranded cotton sew radiating lines of varying lengths from pearls out. Surround pearls with clear beads and then sew them in randomly scattered positions on white spot and outwards to tips of some lines as shown. For gold spots sew beads around edges first and then as shown. Treat tiny spots with no ribbon in similar fashion to large white spot with lines and beads. Tighten material in frame and finish back.

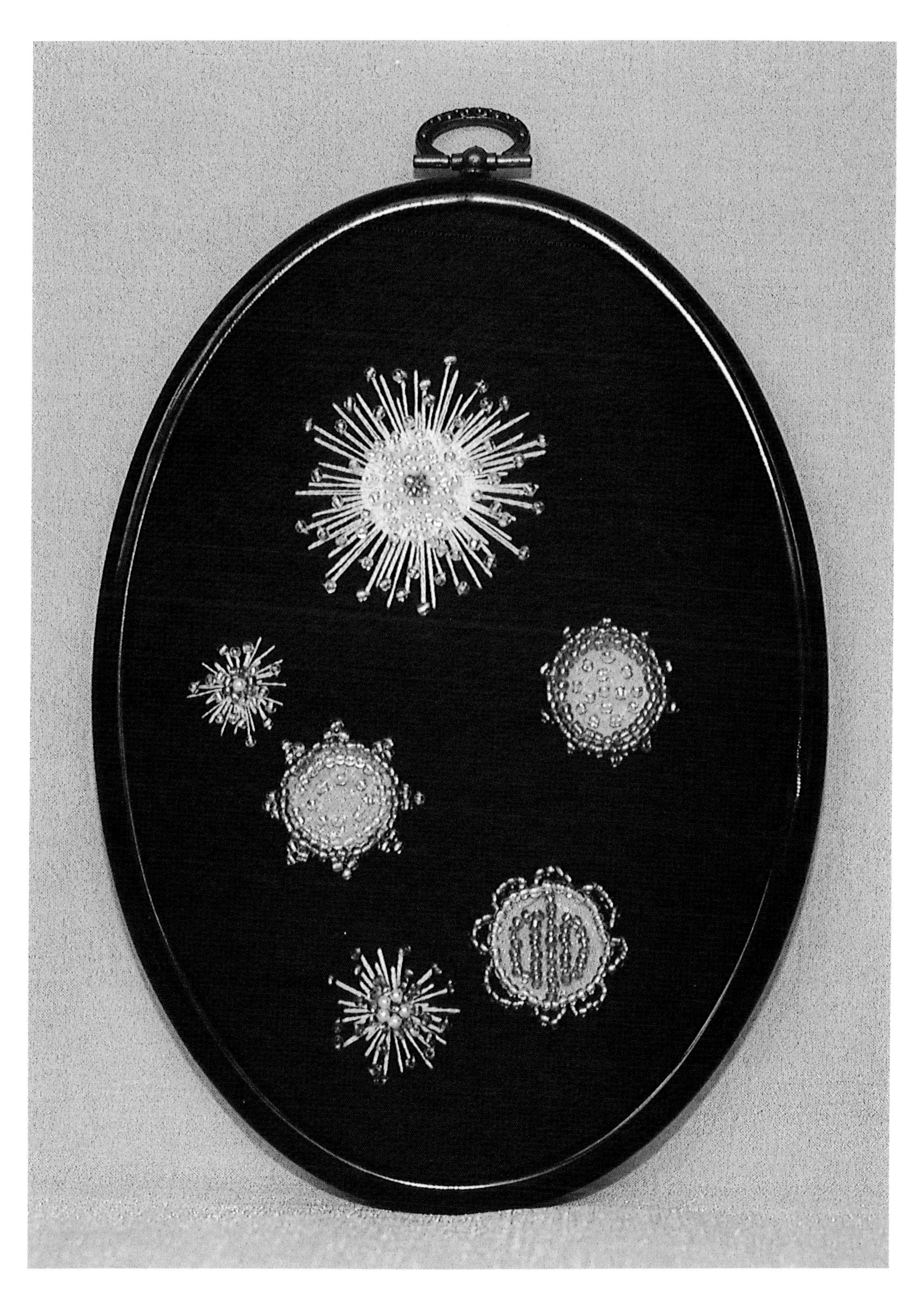

Beaded floral design

For this design choose a piece of firm floral fabric that appeals to you with a medallion or group of flowers that will fit into a frame. I used a pretty piece of furnishing fabric under a piece of voile. The flowers were outlined with matching beads using silver thread and one bead to every second back-stitch. The design was extended outwards a little with further beaded outlines. Most leaves were beaded as well as the black and green centres. Clear translucent beads follow some meandering lines to give extra sparkle.

Plain fabric with the design traced and painted will also give a most attractive result.

You will need:

16.5 cm plastic frame
Firm floral fabric or white linen cut 4 cm larger all round than frame
Piece of voile the same size
Tiny beads to match
Silver thread
Fabric paints

If using plain rather than floral fabric, first trace design on to the white linen. Mix suitable pale colours in fabric paint and apply with a ½″ flat brush. Allow to dry, and iron well while face down on brown paper to fix colour.

Lay voile over the floral fabric or painted linen and place in frame carefully, centring design. Outline flowers with matching beads using silver thread and one bead to every second backstitch. Use green beads for leaves and green and black for centres. Add some meandering lines of your own with clear translucent beads if liked. Tighten material in frame, gather, pad and secure back and finish with felt.

Oriental design

You will need:

21.5 cm wooden embroidery hoop
Blue-green slub taffeta cut into a 32 cm circle
White lawn the same size for lining
3 cm wide red satin ribbon
Gold patterned silk fabric
16 mm golden yellow ribbon
Gold and black beads

Trace design and, using a thin wooden skewer, make holes in paper where corners and points occur. Place design on coloured taffeta and with a white pencil make marks on material through holes. Cut a template for the curved shape in thin cardboard and use to cut shapes from red and gold material.

Bond these shapes to transfer fusing web and arrange in position on design, matching corners

with white pencil marks. Place Glad Bake carefully over top and iron on. Cut squares from gold ribbon and clip notches into them as shown. Bond these to web also, arrange in spaces between pattern and iron on in the same way.

Lay taffeta and lawn together. Place work in frame and sew black beads around the red satin pieces and gold beads around the gold, using back stitching.

Pull work tight in frame, tighten screw and secure back. Do not apply felt if frame is to be bound until after binding is done. Tighten screw again and tie on bow.

Waterlilies

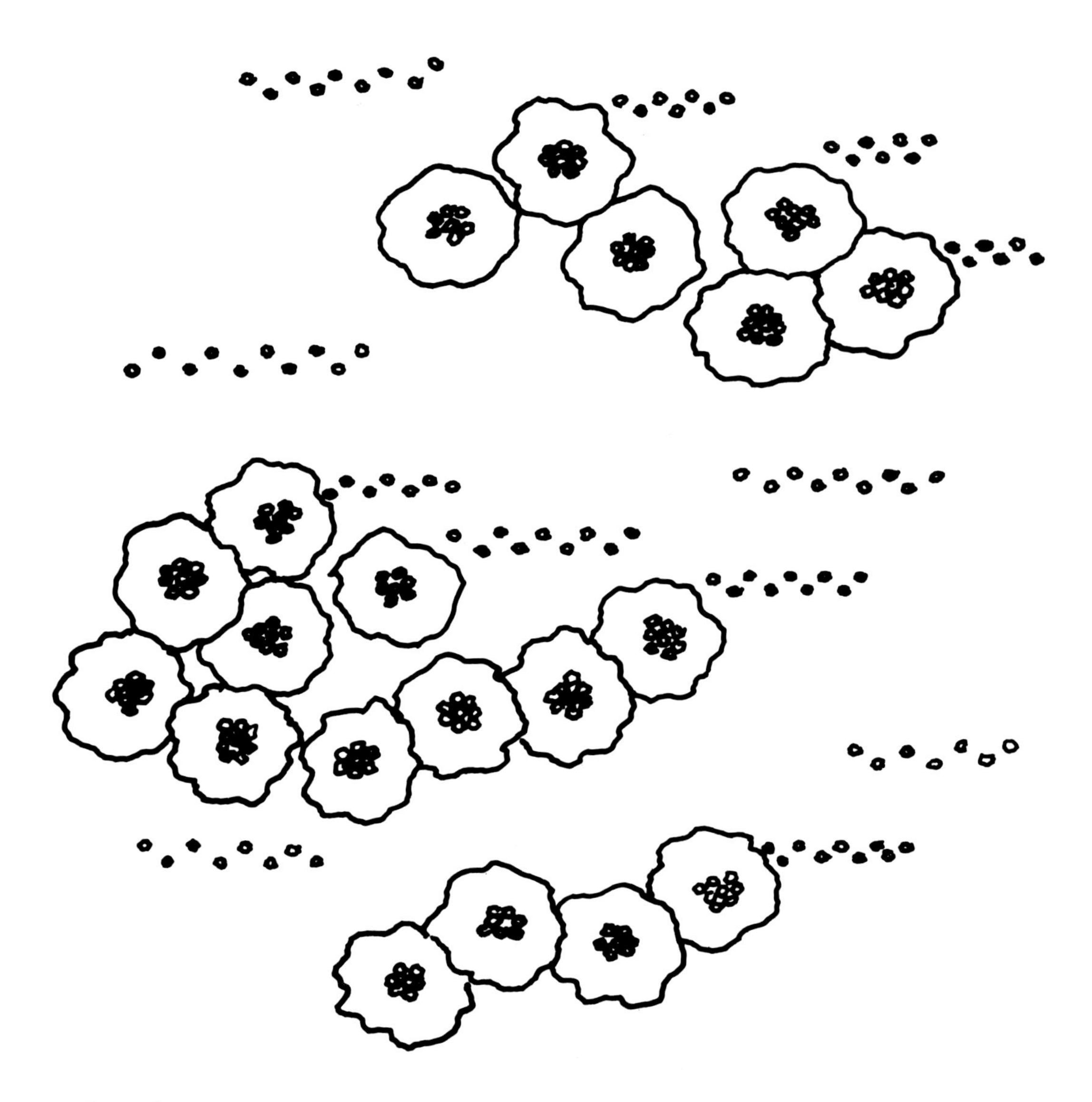

You will need:

18.5 cm wooden embroidery hoop
Grey cotton fabric cut 5 cm larger than hoop all round
Fabric paint
7 mm satin ribbon in pink, white, cream and green
Gold, green and clear beads
Ribbon for binding and bow

With fabric paint mix several shades of blue and blue-green. Apply palest colour to material with a wide flat brush. Finish with streaks of darker colours using edge of brush. Allow to dry and iron well on wrong side over brown paper to fix colour.

Flowers are best not traced onto fabric but centres only marked.

Place material in frame. Cut satin ribbon into 5 cm pieces. Gather along one edge with a matching thread, secure with a couple of tiny stitches and secure join also. Repeat this with all pieces of ribbon and sew in position on fabric. Fill centres of flowers with gold beads and centres of leaves with green. Use green and clear beads to suggest sunshine on water.

Tighten material in frame, tighten screw, pad, gather and secure back. Remove from frame for binding. Return to frame, tighten screw, glue on felt and tie bow to screw to cover.

Paisley

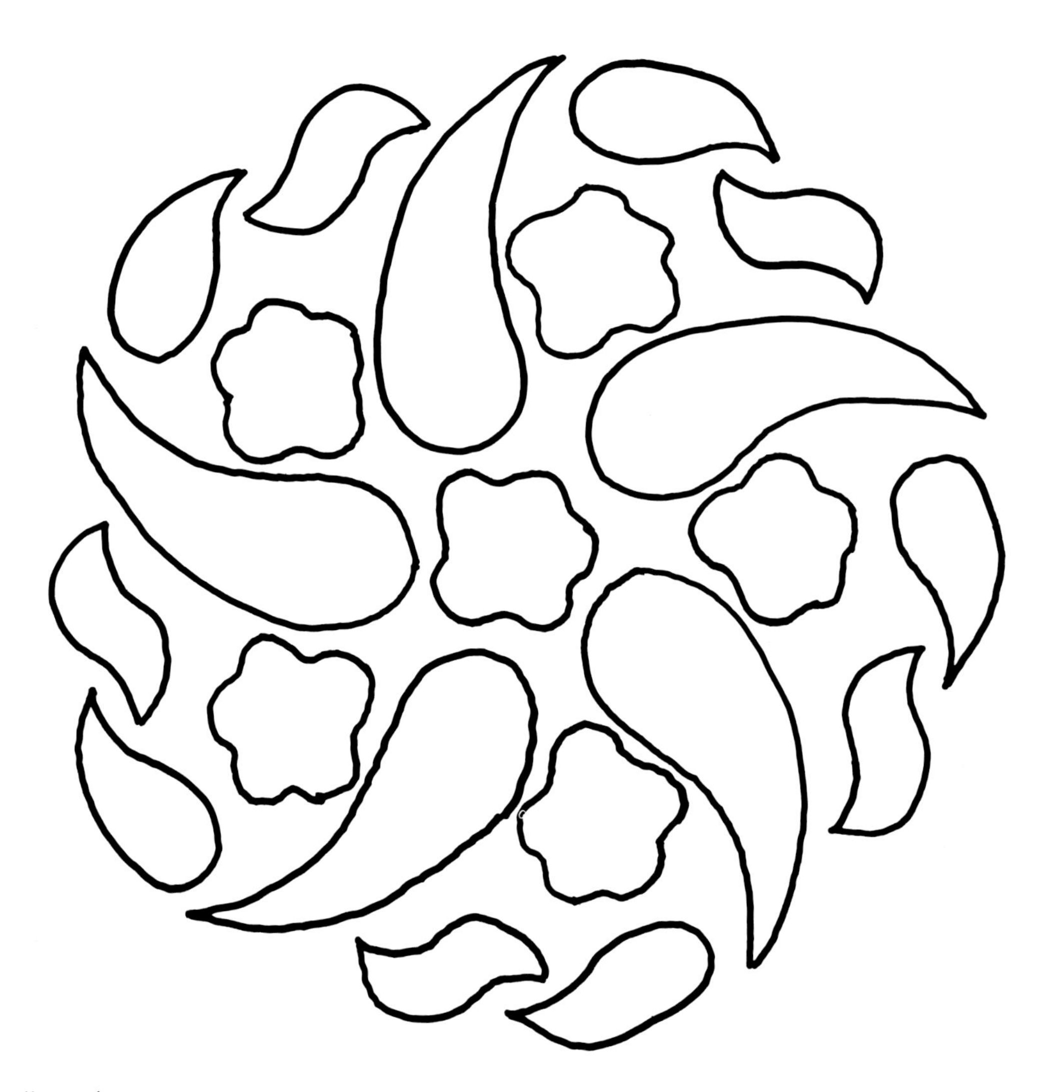

You will need:

16.5 cm wooden embroidery frame
Fine blue linen fabric cut 5 cm larger than hoop all round
White lawn the same size for lining
Fabric paints
3 mm satin ribbon in light and dark blue, pink, white and green
Stranded cottons to match
Beads—dark blue, light blue, green, pink and red
3 metres of 16 mm satin ribbon for binding frame and for bow

Trace design, pin to fabric, slip graphite paper shiny side down in between and trace on, being careful not to smudge graphite on material.

Mix a darker shade of blue and paint the areas suggested in the photograph, then pink areas and red areas, keeping within the lines. When dry, iron on back over brown paper. Put in frame. Backstitch around each part of design with two strands of white stranded cotton.

Sew flowers and leaves in 3 mm ribbon in straight stitches left a little bit loose. Backstitch tiny stems.

Using matching thread (two strands of stranded cotton) bead around each section of pattern with one backstitch between beads. Use a pink bead in the centre of each pink or white flower, green in pale blue flowers and blue in dark blue flowers.

Tighten material in frame, finish work on back but do not glue on felt. Remove from frame to do binding. Return to frame, tighten screw, glue on felt and tie bow to cover screw.

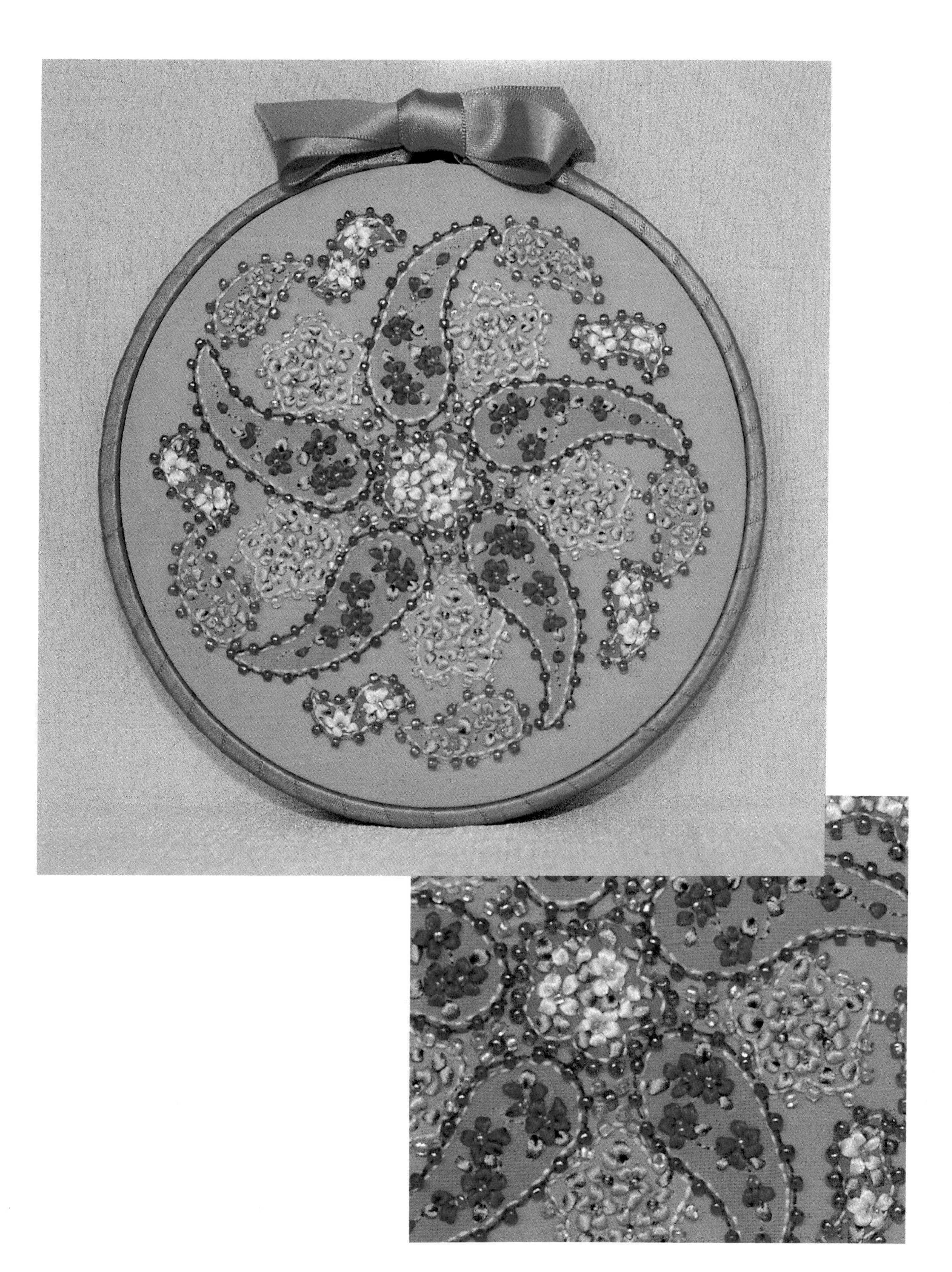

Folded roses

You will need:

12 cm round plastic frame
Linen cut 4 cm larger all round than frame
Fabric paints
6 mm satin ribbon in pink, mauve, green and violet

Using fabric paint, mix pretty pink, turquoise and mauve colours and paint fabric. Allow to dry and iron the back over brown paper to fix colour.

Put linen into frame. Make folded roses, following instructions on page 13. Apply traced design using graphite paper shiny side down. Sew roses in position and make leaves with straight stitches. Backstitch stems with green silk or cotton. Tighten material in frame and finish back.

Pink daisies

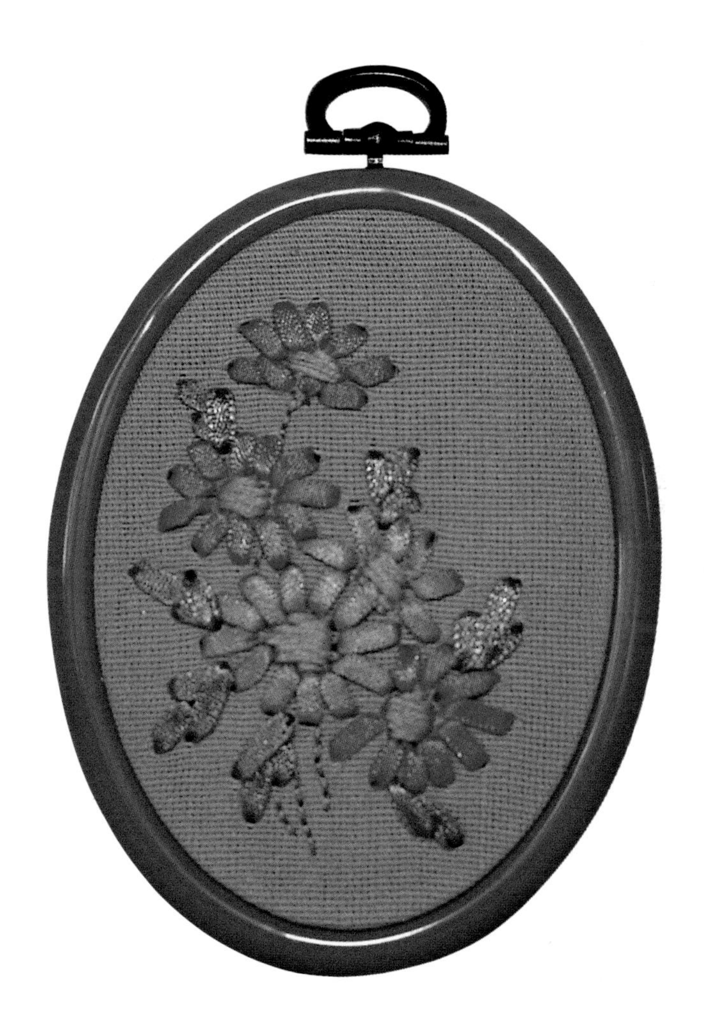

You will need:

10 × 7.5 cm plastic frame
Grey cotton fabric cut 3 cm larger all round than frame
3 mm satin ribbon in two pinks and green
Stranded cotton to match

Trace design and transfer to material using graphite paper shiny side down. Sew ribbon daisies with straight stitches and then make the leaves with overlapping straight stitches. For centres use satin stitch with stranded cotton. Stems are backstitched. Tighten material in frame and finish back.

Blue daisies with yellow creeper

You will need:

10 × 7.5 cm plastic frame
Off-white crinkle polyester cut 3 cm larger all round than frame
White lawn cut same size
3 mm silk ribbon in pale and dark blue, yellow and green

Lay polyester and lawn together and place in frame. Lightly apply traced design, using graphite paper shiny side down.

Sew ribbon daisies with pale blue straight stitches with dark blue over the pale blue as shown. Backstitch stems with two strands of stranded cotton. Leaves are straight stitches in green. Sew yellow French knots in flower centres and on creeper stems. Tighten material in frame and finish back.

Red and pink ribbon roses with daisies

You will need:

10 × 7.5 cm plastic frame
Fine cream linen cut 3 cm larger all around than frame
White lawn cut the same size
3 mm satin ribbon in red, two pinks, cream, blue and green
Stranded cottons to match

Lay linen and lawn together and put into frame. Trace design onto linen using graphite paper shiny side down.

Using two strands of stranded cotton and fly stitch, make base for a ribbon rose. Bring ribbon up close to centre and weave over and under until cotton is covered. Repeat for other roses. Daisies are made with straight stitches and a short green stitch in each centre. Sew leaves with straight stitches and then use two strands of cotton for stems. Tiny blue flowers are made with French knots. Tighten material in frame and finish back.

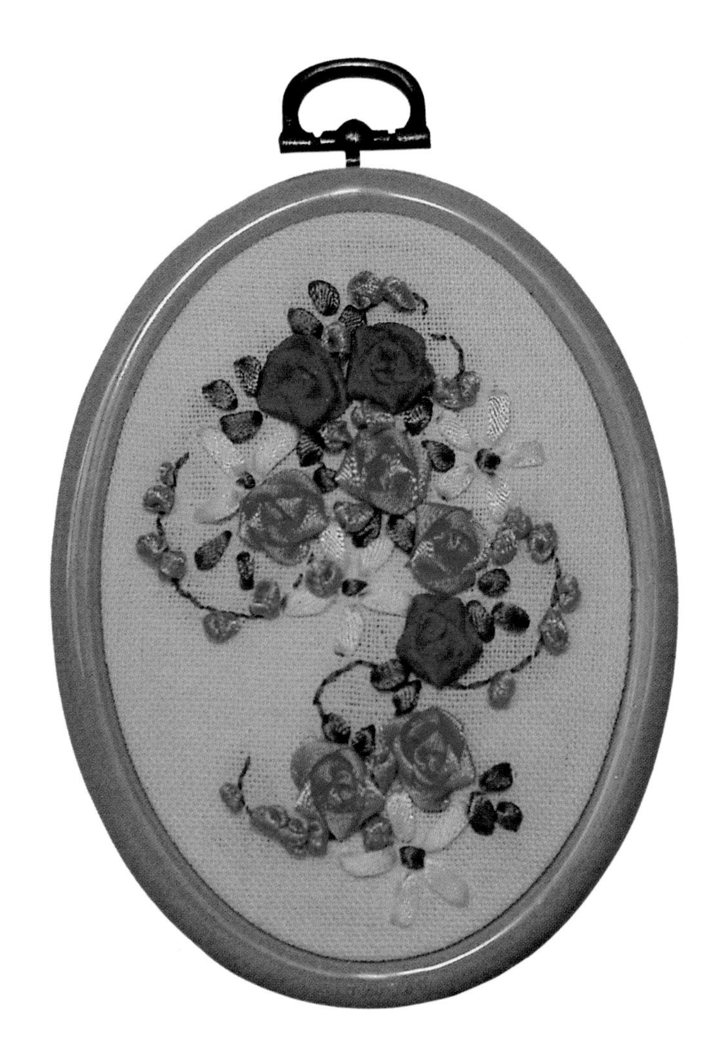

A cluster of crosses

You will need:

11.5 × 15.5 cm plastic frame
Fine linen cut 4 cm larger all round than frame
3 mm silk ribbon in light and dark pink and pale blue
Deep pink stranded cotton
Silver thread
Fabric paints

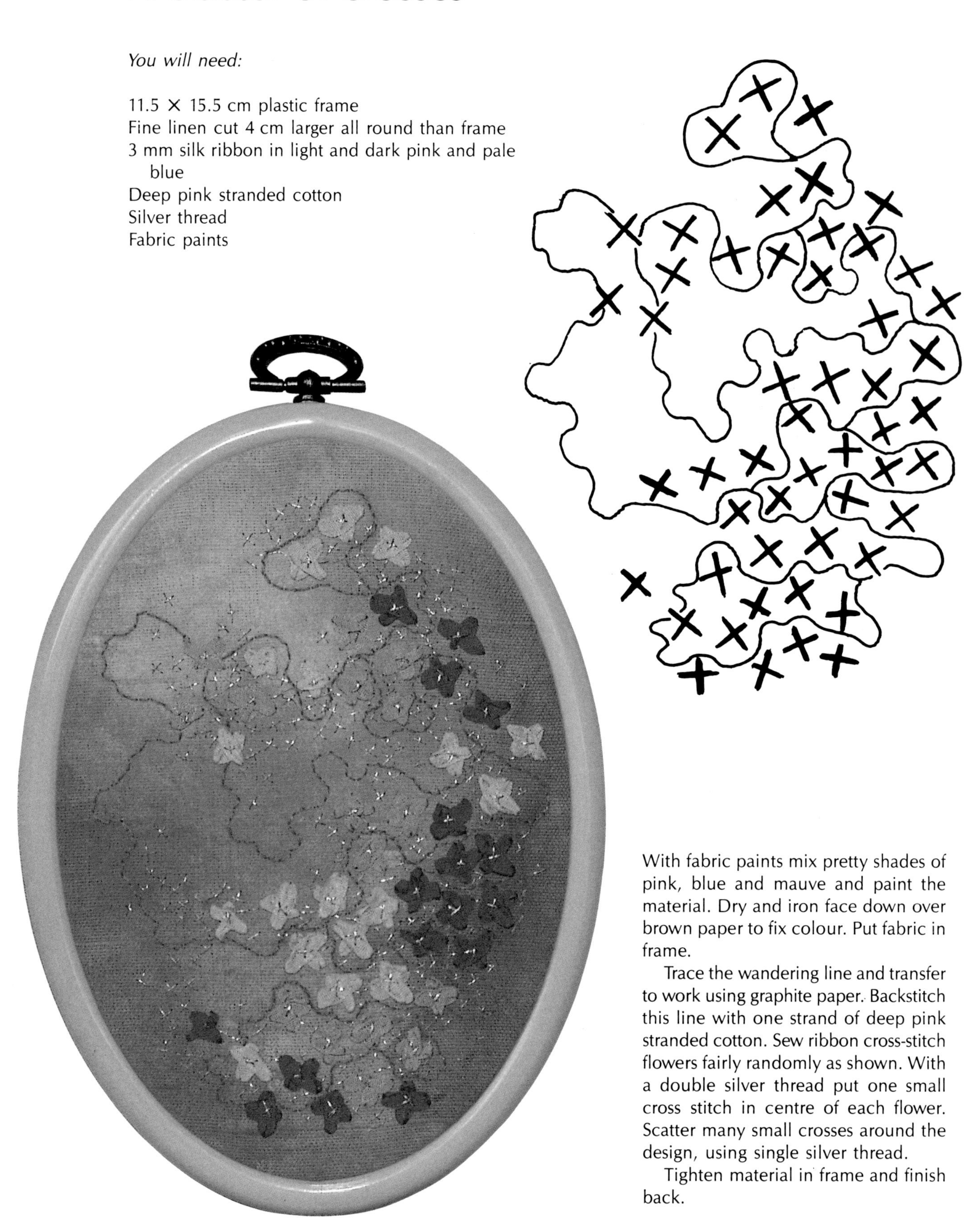

With fabric paints mix pretty shades of pink, blue and mauve and paint the material. Dry and iron face down over brown paper to fix colour. Put fabric in frame.

Trace the wandering line and transfer to work using graphite paper. Backstitch this line with one strand of deep pink stranded cotton. Sew ribbon cross-stitch flowers fairly randomly as shown. With a double silver thread put one small cross stitch in centre of each flower. Scatter many small crosses around the design, using single silver thread.

Tighten material in frame and finish back.

Web design

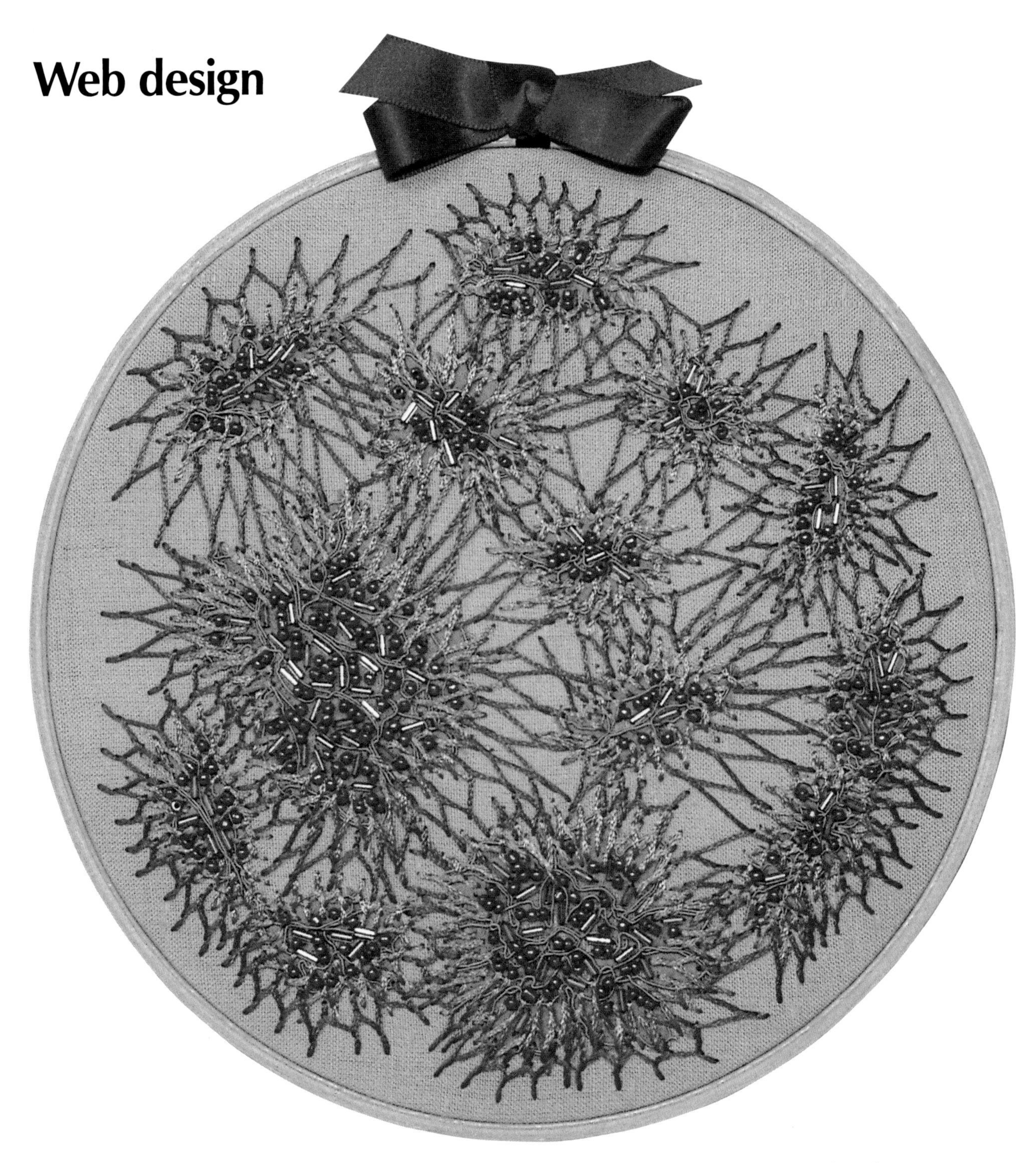

You will need:

21.5 cm wooden embroidery hoop
Fine linen cut 6 cm larger all round than hoop
White lawn the same size for lining
Needlerun or other lace medallions
Red and pink embroidery silk
Red beads and silver bugle beads
17 mm satin ribbon for bow (dark red)

Put fabric in frame and pin medallions in place. Sew medallions to fabric with random length Cretan stitches in pink silk. Darker silk and longer stitches were used to link the medallions together. Stitch silver bugle beads and red beads to the medallions. Tighten fabric in frame, tighten screw and finish back. Tie on red bow to cover screw.

No diagram is given for this pattern as the lace medallions will vary in shape depending on what is available to you. The two rows of stitching around each medallion will also vary according to the medallions' shapes.

Gerberas

You will need:

16.5 cm wooden embroidery hoop
Grey cotton fabric cut into circle 5 cm larger all round than frame
Fabric paints
3 mm satin ribbon in pink, red, cream, yellow and green
Red and yellow beads
16 mm yellow ribbon for bow

Paint fabric in fairly random manner, with yellow and reddish-pink patches where flowers are to go. Allow to dry and iron face down on brown paper to fix colour.

Trace design on material and place in frame. Stitch flowers using darker colours and random length stitches, and leaving a 1 cm circular space for centres. Use paler colours for shorter petals over and in between as shown in the photograph. With pink embroidery silk backstitch around random

patches of background colour. Sew beads around flower centres also in a random manner. Green ribbon stems are fixed in place with very tiny stitches at intervals along each side.

Tighten material in frame and tighten screw. Finish back and tie on bow to cover screw.